Congress Warned Over Russia

The smell of war is in the air.
What can Congress do?

William Dunkerley

Published by
Omnicom Press
New Britain, CT, USA
Publishers since 1981

www.OmnicomPress.com

ISBN-13: 978-1979534932
ISBN-10: 1979534934
Printed in the United States of America

Congress Warned Over Russia *is part of the "Russia: Straight Talk on Hushed Issues" monograph series. It is dedicated to the concept of a safe, sustaining, and positive relationship between the United States and the Russian Federation.*

A list of other monographs in this series can be found at:

www.OmnicomPress.com/monographs

CONTENTS

Chapter 1
NONSENSICAL BABBLE

Standing up to alleged Russian aggression was a central theme of a June 14, 2016 hearing of the House Foreign Affairs Committee. Chairman Ed Royce set the tone: "From invading Ukraine to bombing Syrian hospitals and schools, Putin has only become more belligerent, in part due to a lack of US leadership and credibility. We must work with Russia from a position of strength."

Committee members heard testimony from former ambassador Michael McFaul, former American ambassador to the Soviet Union Jack Matlock, and American NGO official Leon Aron. Congress members also presented their own views, as well as questioning the distinguished witnesses.

I watched these proceedings with great interest,

and formed an impression of the overall tenor of the discourse. Sadly, I must say, that it predominantly sounded like the babble of persons who are either badly misinformed or attempting to deceive Americans by presenting specious information. The job of untangling and debunking all that nonsense is more than what can reasonably be undertaken for now. To me the takeaway is the realization of how many American lawmakers espouse views that are almost totally unsupported by facts.

Two speakers distinguished themselves by deviating from that nonsense: Ambassador Matlock and Representative Dana Rohrabacher. They were able to present wise perspectives that were not based upon fallacious precepts. The others didn't look as sane.

Chapter 2
CONGRESSIONAL CORONARY

Representative Gerry Connolly (D-VA-11) appeared agitated to the verge of seizure while hyping alarming allegations about Russia. I saw him gripping his chest and gasping for air, looking like he was on the brink of a medical crisis.

But he was not. Connolly was just deeply distressed during the hearing over the trouble he believes Russia is causing in the world.

Clearly this is a highly-charged hyperemotional issue for Connolly. You see it in his face and gestures.

It also came out in his verbal inflection. Each time he said "Russian" he didn't simply say the word. It came out with a distinct tinge of deep disgust as "RrrUSHan!"

In making his points about the Ukraine crisis he said people there are dying because of "RrrUSHan! provocations," "RrrUSHan! subterfuge," and "RrrUSHan! provocateurs."

Chapter 3
OFF THE DEEP END

If you delve into Connolly's understanding of Russia, the reason behind his unbridled angst becomes clear.

In a C-Span interview earlier, Connolly took to the soapbox about the Ukraine crisis of 2014. He likened Russia's role to that of Nazi Germany's in the occupation of the Sudetenland. Connolly exclaimed; "Had we responded to naked aggression it would have set some limits and some clear stakes for Hitler and his band of thugs!"

Connolly went on to explain: "Now here we are in Europe and we are seeing naked aggression ... by the Russian military ... and we have to set limits." He believes that Putin must be punished and that "part of that punishment has to be a military calculation."

Back at the House hearing, Connolly continued that theme: "Putin seems to be engaged in some kind of reestablishment of Russian hegemony in some kind of delusional tsarist longing for some glorious past that really never existed. And that's very dangerous."

I think Connolly's rhetoric is very dangerous.

Chapter 4
CONNOLLY SHOT DOWN

During the House hearing Connolly turned to
Michael McFaul, former Ambassador to Moscow
and a witness at the hearing. The congressman
was looking for support on his thesis about
Russia's action in Ukraine.

But instead he got pulled up short. McFaul
clearly asserted: "It was not, in my view, some
grand design to recreate the Soviet Union."

What's more, McFaul said of the Russian activity
in Ukraine: "It was in response to the collapse of
the government in Kiev."

That completely shot down Connolly's theory
that Putin is bent on making a Hitlerian march to
conquer former Soviet space. Hooray to McFaul
for setting the record straight.

But Connelly didn't give up even then. He recounted the sense of the "RrrUSHan!" problem he got from people in Ukraine, the Baltics, Kyrgyzstan, Mongolia, and Georgia. He added, "I think there is real anxiety among lots of former Eastern European countries, and they're looking to our leadership to try to respond to it."

I don't doubt there is heightened anxiety in those areas.

But I'd attribute it to the rantings and unsubstantiated allegations of troublemakers like Connelly. They're likely the source of the anxiety. And they're the ones that are pushing and pushing world tensions toward the brink.

I wonder, do the constituents who sent Connolly to Washington realize what he's up to? I understand he's running unopposed for reelection next time!

Chapter 5
WARNING TO CONGRESS

In advance of the hearing I was invited by Congressman Dana Rohrabacher to submit a statement to be included in the official record of the hearing. It is reprinted below:

Before the House Committee on Foreign Affairs

Hearing on US Policy Toward Putin's Russia

June 14, 2016

Statement of
William Dunkerley

--Expert on Russia's Media Sector and on the Credibility of America's Media Coverage of Russia and Its Leaders

[Summary: Both US and Russian leaders demonstrably engage in formulating policy based on misinformation and consequent misunderstanding. This creates a tense and dangerous situation. It also forecloses opportunities for reasonable dialogue and constructive cooperation. A practical plan is offered for disrupting this problematic negative trajectory in relations.]

My name is William Dunkerley. I am a media business analyst and organization development expert based in New Britain, CT.

I have extensive in-country experience in analyzing Russian media organizations from top to bottom and in investigating the credibility demonstrated by American media organizations in covering important issues regarding Russia and its leaders. I have several affiliations that are detailed in an appended bio.

Thank you for the opportunity to introduce evidence on the prospects for redirecting today's vitriolic and contentious US-Russia relationship toward areas of productive cooperation.

For many, such a redirection may seem as attainable as finding the end of a rainbow. Every week a battle rages in the media in which

America expresses alarm over Russian international aggression and antidemocratic policies at home. In turn Russia expresses alarm over an overbearing US role in the world that includes threats to Russia's security.

My own research and analysis has shown that both sides are pursuing policies that contain a strong element of misunderstanding. I've found that this misunderstanding is propagated to a great extent by misinformation found in the media of the respective countries.

The award winning Stanford University professor emeritus Martin Hellman wrote: "The more I study Russian-American relations, the more potential I see for a misunderstanding to escalate into a crisis, and the more concerned I become about the world's nuclear complacency. I sometimes feel like a German Jew in the early 1930s who has read Mein Kampf and tries in vane to alert his countrymen to the need for taking action before it's too late."

I share Hellman's perception of the dangerous potential of entrenched misunderstanding, and strongly believe it mandatory for the Congress to play a leadership role in diverting us from the current perilous trajectory of our approach to Russia.

I will propose a clear and practical plan for accomplishing that. But first I'd like to expand briefly on the facts about the mutual misunderstanding:

For me the misinformation alarm sounded in early 2000. News stories were proliferating that lamented Vladimir Putin's crackdown on Russia's free press. A February 16, 2000 Reuters report headlined, "Journalists say Russia press freedom at risk."

The flaw in that story is that Putin had inherited no free press on which to crack down. I knew that from personal experience with indigenous media organizations. The press freedom story is a fraud perpetrated by two oligarchs. They were engaged in nefarious activities that were frowned upon by Putin. Seeking an upper hand in the matter they used the trumped-up press freedom allegations to compromise him. They were simply seeking an advantage over Putin to protect their own interests. Few people saw through the ruse.

The truth is that Yeltsin era laws precluded the profitability of media outlets. They never had the financial independence to serve their audiences honestly and freely. Their bankrupt condition led them into subjugation by oligarchs, state and private enterprises, governors, mayors, legislators, and even the Kremlin. They all put money into the loss-making media enterprises in return for the ability to color the news to their own favor. I estimate that at least eighty percent of the media were then under the control of some level of government. Close to zero percent were free to reliably tell their audiences the truth.

As a means for citizens to be informed and exercise vigilance over their government, Russia's media were abject failures. Observers who believed the bogus crack-down story had looked only at surface appearances. They seemed oblivious to the fundamental realities, and therefore came to totally unwarranted conclusions. They misunderstood the actual realities. I give greater detail on this consequential problem in my book *Medvedev's Media Affairs*.

The fraudulent tale about press freedom's doom is actually prologue to many stories that were to come afterwards.

In early 2007 the International Federation of Journalists commissioned me to study and report on media coverage of the November 2006 polonium poisoning of Alexander Litvinenko. My report to the organization's World Congress documented that the mainstream story accusing Putin of culpability was another fabrication. It was perpetrated convincingly by political enemies of Putin's. Their admitted ultimate aim was to destabilize Russia, foment a violent revolution, and institute a monarchy. That presumably would put them back in control.

Yet still today, after all the foregoing has been publically revealed, the fabrication is regarded not only as the truth, but as proof positive of Putin's criminal modus operandi. I don't know whether or not Putin was involved in Litvinenko's death. My research neither implicates nor exonerates him. But I have proved that those who concocted and advanced that story were lying. This is a very massive and sophisticated scheme that successfully bamboozled the world. I've written two books to document all the details. They are titled *The Phony Litvinenko Murder*, and *Litvinenko Murder Case Solved*.

The widespread misunderstanding created by these misinformation campaigns has led to a serious and untoward consequence. It is a phenomenon known as "confirmation bias." This is a psychological term for people's tendency to interpret information in ways that are in harmony with their existing beliefs, expectations, or hypotheses. It turns out the persistently phony Russia stories have spawned reactions at that level of unshakable belief.

According to Tufts University research professor Raymond S. Nickerson: "If one were to attempt to identify a single problematic aspect of human reasoning that deserves attention above all others, the 'confirmation bias' would have to be among the candidates for consideration. Many have written about this bias, and it appears to be sufficiently strong and pervasive that one is led to wonder whether the bias, by itself, might account for a significant fraction of the disputes, altercations, and misunderstandings that occur among individuals, groups, and nations." Indeed: disputes among nations.

What this means is when information confirms existing beliefs, it results in assigning credibility to that information, even if there is no apparent substantiation. Things that fly in the face of pre-existing expectations tend to be disbelieved.

This is a problem that must be addressed if any significant progress is to be achieved in promoting positive cooperation between the United States and Russia. I strongly urge that Congress address how to disrupt the dangerous downward spiral that's put a death lock on current relations.

Lamentably the information pool about Russia has become so polluted by maliciously-inspired misinformation that we need to start anew in our understanding the country and its leadership.

To that end I wish to advance the following solution:

Congress needs and deserves information on current events that is devoid of confirmation bias. It's been demonstrated that it cannot get that from the Western media, or from governmental, partisan, or commercial sources that have an axe to grind and benefactors to please. Something new is desperately needed.

I recommend establishing a commission comprised exclusively of citizen members that have the skill and expertise to validate or discredit news reports and to supply Congress with authoritative and confidential disclosures.

The commission would function in the realm of observable facts and realism, and not in the domain of ideology. It would be precluded from offering policy advice, and mandated to deal with just the facts on which members of Congress can base their own informed judgments.

Congress should invite Russia as well to set up a counterpart commission so that Russian leaders can have the benefit of their own reality-based information in a similar way.

I realize that the establishment of such a commission would face some critical obstacles. One for instance involves the need to avoid politicization and loading the commission with ideologues. But I have in mind ways to overcome this and other challenges. I'd be pleased to work with Congressional representatives in structuring the commission appropriately.

The United States and Russia are the two nuclear superpowers that uniquely possess the capability to pose an existential threat to human civilization as we know it. This is far too serious a matter to abandon sensibility to reckless partisan or ideological differences. The proposed commission will serve to weed through deceptive media rhetoric, thus avoiding false points of contention. It is our best bet for disrupting the desperate course of deteriorating relations. I urge prompt action on this important matter before it's too late.

Bio:

William Dunkerley is an expert on Russia's

media sector and on the credibility of American media coverage of Russia and it leaders.

Mr. Dunkerley has worked to remediate the very challenging problems that face Russian media organizations. His work has been supported by various American organizations and agencies. He personally conducted intensive interventions in 17 different Russian cities. Through his seminars he has worked with hundreds of Russian media managers literally from Kaliningrad to Kamchatka. He is author of a book about Russia's media milieu, and has written dozens of articles about Russian media management. He served as principal consultant to the Publishers and Editors Association of Russia.

He also has done intensive work in Bulgaria, Romania, Hungary, Czech Republic, Latvia, and Croatia. In both Croatia and Russia his invited advice to governmental leaders has been incorporated into their countries' laws governing the media. In 2006 Mr. Dunkerley delivered a keynote address on the prospects for press freedom in Russia at the World Congress of the World Association of Newspapers.

Mr. Dunkerley has also closely studied the American media's coverage of Russia and its leaders. In 2007 he was commissioned by the

International Federation of Journalists to analyze and report on the Western media coverage of the Alexander Litvinenko polonium death case.

He is now the author of three books and hundreds of magazine and newspaper articles dealing with the problematic aspects of Western media coverage of Russian issues.

Mr. Dunkerley is principal of William Dunkerley Publishing Consultants, editor and publisher of *Editors Only*, a monthly for newspaper and magazine editors, and of *STRAT*, a monthly publication on digital and print magazine strategies. He has served as a columnist for the *Moscow Times*, *SREDA* (Russia's first media management magazine), and *Komsomolskaya Pravda* (Russia's largest newspaper). He is also a Senior Fellow at the American University in Moscow.

Note: See *Guardian* article titled "Six Reasons You Can't Take the Litvinenko Report Seriously" here. http://bit.ly/1LhhFJ3

Chapter 6
EPILOGUE

Looking back over all this, I am struck by the contrast between the "nonsensical babble" of most speakers at the hearing, and the minority voices of sanity.

The babblers argue for dangerous confrontation between the United States and Russia on issues that lack any demonstrable factual basis.

Let's examine the counterpoints raised by Ambassador Matlock and Congressman Rohrabacher.

Ambassador Matlock

--"The number of nuclear weapons that remain in Russian and US arsenals represent a potential existential threat to every nation on earth.

--"We could not fight each other without committing suicide."

He asked what rational leader would intend to do that.

Matlock went on,

--"Nuclear cooperation with Russia has deteriorated and seems practically nonexistent. It is urgent to restore that cooperation if we are to inhibit future proliferation. We're unlikely to do so if we proceed with plans to increase our military presence in Eastern Europe."

But that's exactly what those with fabricated indictments of Russia want. Many support placing lethal weaponry along Russia's borders.

Matlock then offers a more constructive approach,

--"Now if there is any issue in which the United States and Russia have common interest it is in fighting terrorism. They're more vulnerable than we are. Sometimes we tend to forget that, and I still don't understand why we've not been able to have more effective cooperation.

--"So I think the main thing we need to bear in

mind is that in confronting these things, whether it be terrorism, failed states, organized crime, environmental degradation, US and Russian basic interests are not in conflict. As we deal with them, as we must, Russia will be either part of the problem or part of the solution. It's obviously in our interests to do what we can to encourage Russia to join us in confronting them. They're unlikely to do so if they regard us as an enemy or a competitor for influence in their neighborhood.

--"We can argue about who is more responsible for this situation but the fact is that as you well know politics is driven by perceptions, and [Russian] perceptions are that we have been consistently moving against their interests and trying to encircle them and even trying to interfere in their internal politics."

At this point Chairman Royce brought down the gavel on Matlock!

Matlock's facts were conflicting with the mainstream narrative. That was apparently too much for Royce to allow. Earlier the ambassador pointed out that "The perceptions on both sides have distortions." Now Matlock was pointing to the role played by the United States in the US-Russia rift.

As Matlock continued speaking, the chairman continued to interrupt and silence him. What a shameful display that was.

(Note: A complete transcript of this hearing can be found in my monograph titled *US Policy toward Putin's Russia: A hearing before the House Committee on Foreign Affairs*.)

Congressman Rohrabacher

"The fact is there has been an unrelenting hostility toward Russia from the very days that we were negotiating with them and they were making concessions that led to tearing down the Berlin Wall.

"Just let me note ... our airplanes right now ... are being buzzed by Russian airplanes, our ships. The American people see that. Well, where are our ships? The ship that was being buzzed -- I don't remember where I heard this -- was in the Baltic Sea and here it was, I don't know how many miles from St. Petersburg, but why are we sending our US military forces that close to Russia?

We have nuclear weapons delivery systems that are being aimed at Russia. How else would they think of that except as being a hostile act? And for them to buzz a ship to see what kind of ship it was right off their borders?

"By the way, some of these ships that we have sent there are closer to Russia than Catalina Island is to Los Angeles. What if some nuclear weapons delivery system showed up there? What would we think? Would we send an airplane out to buzz it around and see what kind of ship it is?

"I think that both sides, both Russia and the United States, need to take a deep breath and step back from this whole military operation that is actually making things worse rather than making things better, and we need to find out where our differences are, negotiate them, see where we can work together. "

Is Anybody Listening?

These are very thoughtful and well grounded warnings.

The only question now is whether Congress will have the wisdom to head them.

Appendix I
THE AUTHOR

William Dunkerley is a media business analyst and Senior Fellow at American University in Moscow. He has worked on behalf of US interests in promoting press freedom in Eastern Europe and the former Soviet Union. He was commissioned by the International Federation of Journalists to analyze problems in certain Western press coverage of Russian issues. Mr. Dunkerley has been instrumental in shaping laws governing the media in Eastern Europe and Russia and has offered testimony to the United States Congress on media concerns. He has personally done intensive work in seven post communist countries, including interventions in seventeen different cities across all Russia. He is principal of William Dunkerley Publishing Consultants, and publisher of two industry monthlies, *Editors Only* and the *STRAT* newsletter.

Appendix II
THIS SERIES

"Russia: Straight Talk on Hushed Issues" is a monograph series that looks behind the popular headlines and presents iconoclastic analyses. The books explain aspects of mainstream news that are either being distorted, glossed over, or hushed up.

The etiology of these media distortions is complex. Historically there was little harshness in the coverage of Yeltsin's misdeeds, perhaps a result of Western giddiness over the collapse of the Soviet Union.

When Putin entered the scene in 1999 the kid gloves came off. He was demonized. Russian tycoons who had been involved in skullduggery under Yeltsin found the new leader problematic.

Boris Berezovsky, one of the tycoons, carried

media attacks to new heights after fleeing to London in 2001 to evade corruption charges. He packaged and distributed highly engaging news stories with associated graphics and interview opportunities to media outlets worldwide. Probably because of that convenience, they were readily accepted by the media unquestioningly despite their lack of factual bases.

Inexplicably, after Berezovsky's 2014 death, the stream of demonizing stories continued. Had Berezovsky's campaign just made an indelible impression that still taints the views of media and political leaders in the US and elsewhere? Or is there a new kingpin yet to be identified?

Regardless, many people have indeed formed beliefs based on the prevalence of distorted news and are committed to them. It would be unrealistic to think many of these folks will accept any contravening facts and analyses.

So the intention of this series is to give open-minded audiences in the US and other Western countries insights into misleading and fabricated reportage. That should allow them to arrive at more realistic and fact-based understandings, thus facilitating their serving more responsibly as members of our society. The intention is not to exonerate anyone who has been accused, but to point out that the accusers are liars and fabricators. (Note: Monographs in this series appear in no particular order.)

H.G. Wells once said: "Civilization is in a race between education and catastrophe."

But what is now unfolding in the theater of US-Russia relations is a race between catastrophe and utter disaster.

One entrant is the United States, and the other is Russia. Which country is on which side actually makes no difference. In this race, there are allegations, then sanctions, and then retributions for the previous actions. It is a self perpetuating loop.

This is a race in which the winner will personify either political buffoonery or plain stupidity. And which of the two is the victor will also make no difference. The main point for the rest of us is that this race will cause us all to lose.

As part of the "Russia: Straight Talk on Hushed Issues" monograph series, this book is dedicated to ending that foolish race, and to the concept of a safe, sustaining, and positive relationship between the United States and the Russian Federation.

Appendix III
ACKNOWLEDGMENT

In the face of much media misinformation about
Russia, I wish to acknowledge the effort and
perseverance of all who have spoken and written
the honest truth. They have shown great courage
in bucking the unfortunate mainstream trend
toward fabrication. Their work serves as an
essential predicate to this book. --W.D.

www.ingramcontent.com/pod-product-compliance
Lightning Source LLC
Chambersburg PA
CBHW061927270726
48660CB00003BA/1033